INFO TeCH

Series Editor: Sue Hewer

D1102220

6

Multimedia in language learning

Paul Slater and Sarah Varney-Burch

INFO TeCH

The views expressed in this publication are the authors' and do not necessarily represent those of CILT.

Acknowledgements

The authors and publisher would like to thank copyright holders for the permission granted to reproduce copyright material, as detailed next to the relevant excerpts.

Special thanks to Ute Hitchin, Sue Hewer, Jane Carne, Tim Jones, Derek Kelly and Elspeth Broady for their support, help and advice.

First published in 2001 by the Centre for Information on Language Teaching and Research, 20 Bedfordbury, Covent Garden, London WC2N 4LB

Copyright © 2001 Centre for Information on Language Teaching and Research

ISBN 1 902031 62 8

2004 2003 2002 2001 / 10 9 8 7 6 5 4 3 2 1

A catalogue record for this book is available from the British Library

Printed in Great Britain by Copyprint UK Ltd

CILT Publications are available from: **Central Books,** 99 Wallis Rd, London E9 5LN. Tel: 020 8986 4854. Fax: 020 8533 5821. Book trade representation (UK and Ireland): **Broadcast Book Services,** Charter House, 27a London Road, Croydon CR0 2RE. Tel: 020 8681 8949. Fax: 020 8688 0615.

Contents

1 Introduction   1
What is multimedia?   1
How is multimedia stored and delivered?   1
When are we able to use multimedia software?   2
What are the benefits of multimedia?   3
Where next?   5

2 Understanding multimedia   6
The features of multimedia   6
Where and when multimedia can be used   8
Planning and organisation – practical considerations   12
Getting started   14
Success   17
The future   17

3 Dedicated multimedia for language learning   20
Categories of material   20
The four skills, grammar and vocabulary   25
Evaluation   32
Availability   36

4 Exploiting authentic material on CD-ROM   37
The advantages of using authentic materials   37
Potential drawbacks   38
Different types of authentic materials   38

5 Teacher- and learner-produced multimedia materials   51
Teacher-produced multimedia materials   51
Learner-produced multimedia work   57

6 Useful lists and information   66
Addresses   66
Useful website addresses   71
Glossary   72
References   74

1 | Introduction

WHAT IS MULTIMEDIA?

Multimedia is made up of a combination of text, pictures, sound, animation and video which are delivered on a computer. Although many language teachers already use multiple media in their lessons in the form of pictures, photos, texts, audio clips and video, this range of media usually requires the use of several pieces of equipment: photocopiers, cassette players, videos, etc. One of multimedia's benefits is that it enables you to give learners access to the same wide range of media through a single piece of equipment, a computer. However, to take advantage of the full potential of multimedia the computer used must be equipped with the necessary components. To be able to hear sound the computer must have a sound card plus speakers or headphones, and to record sound you will need a microphone. The computer must be fitted with a CD-ROM drive, and ideally one of the newer DVD drives.

HOW IS MULTIMEDIA STORED AND DELIVERED?

Since their first appearance, **CD-ROMs** have been synonymous with multimedia. However, CD-ROMs are simply a medium for storing large quantities of the **digital files** of text, picture and other resources that computers need to access in order to display multimedia, and these files can be stored on any disk designed to hold digital information provided it has adequate storage capacity. The types of disks available range from **floppy disks**, which store a relatively small amount of information, to new types of disk, such as **DVDs**, which can hold huge quantities of data. Multimedia can also be accessed across **electronic networks**. For some this will be through the use of a local network linking computers in a class or school; for others, using the **World Wide Web**, it will be across the global computer network called the **Internet**.

WHEN ARE WE ABLE TO USE MULTIMEDIA SOFTWARE?

Use of multimedia in language education is not restricted to language learning packages on CD-ROMs, as there are many other ways of incorporating multimedia into the curriculum. Some of the approaches which we will suggest are more challenging than buying ready made materials on CD-ROM, but trying them out will prove educationally rewarding.

When you want to do something with a computer, you need to decide which computer tool, or **software application**, you need to use to do that work. To write a letter you use a word processor and to create a picture you use a drawing package, but these are just two of the types of software applications available on most computers. The software companies which create these applications now build more multimedia potential into even the most standard application.

If you have access to a word processor running on a computer with the facility to play sound, then you can begin working with multimedia. Word processors on computers now allow you to include not only pictures in your documents, but also sound and video. This means that you can prepare your own materials tailored to your learners' needs which include sound or video support at selected points. Alternatively, pupils can create work with multimedia elements as part of a project. The value of this for pronunciation, speaking, listening, reading and writing activities is significant, and the potential for exploitation is as limitless as our own imagination.

Another way of accessing and creating multimedia which is being used more widely in education is a presentation software. These applications, such as Microsoft's *PowerPoint*, were originally intended for business presentations but are now being used by teachers to give multimedia presentations in classes. Many classic pieces of Computer Assisted Language Learning (CALL) software, such as gap-filling programs and text reconstruction packages, also now incorporate multimedia. For information on this type of package see InfoTech 2, *Text manipulation* by Sue Hewer. Powerful yet easy-to-use multimedia authoring packages are also now available, enabling teachers and learners to

2

INFO TECH

Multimedia in language learning

create more advanced multimedia. The phenomenal growth of the World Wide Web means that a vast choice of on-line multimedia relevant to language learners can now be accessed if you have a connection to the Internet. See InfoTech 3, *WWW The Internet* by Terry Atkinson.

WHAT ARE THE BENEFITS OF MULTIMEDIA?

The hyperbole and exaggeration surrounding multimedia have understandably led to some scepticism from teachers. However, multimedia does have a range of educational benefits which merit attention. These benefits support most of the aspects of language development that teachers have to address, including work on the skills areas, vocabulary development and cultural awareness. The use of multimedia is not tied to any single language teaching approach and can therefore be exploited to support any aspect of the curriculum.

Motivation

Access to multimedia increases learners' motivation. Although the initial appeal of multimedia is almost certainly due to its novelty, teachers and learners soon discover other aspects which are more educationally significant. A rich media environment allows contextualisation of the target language in simulations which learners recognise as having practical real-life applications. The variety of activities, coupled with the rapid feedback that multimedia provides, also help maintain learner interest and attention.

A multisensory learning environment

The range of media available with multimedia enables you to choose the most suitable medium for the specific language elements; work on listening skills can be done by playing recordings on the computer; if reading work is needed, then texts can be presented on screen. A learner facing a new word can see its spelling, hear its pronunciation and see supporting visuals which clarify its meaning. In this way, the use of one medium reinforces what the pupil began learning through another. At its best, interactive multimedia has the potential to create a multisensory learning environment which supports specific learning styles and can be tailored to match individual learners' needs.

3

Controllability and flexibility

Multimedia not only offers you and your learners access to a variety of media, but provides a range and level of control over learning materials not previously available. Computer technology gives you a highly efficient way of managing and presenting the different materials which you use in your teaching. This controllability and flexibility means materials can be tailored to the learning needs of particular classes or groups within classes. It also allows you to allocate work to pupils and monitor their performance while work is being done or after it has been completed.

Interactivity

For learners using multimedia, it is the interactive element that brings them control over the learning environment. Following teacher guidance, interactivity allows the learners to select the materials they need to work with, the order in which they want to work through those materials, and the pace they want to work at. Interactivity also provides the learner with the help, guidance and feedback needed for a successful learning experience. Some learning packages are also designed so that learners must successfully complete activities in order to progress. This encourages active engagement with the materials.

A safe environment

Working with multimedia packages offers a private and forgiving environment which helps to reduce the anxiety that many second language learners experience. This facilitates the type of autonomous language learning which has been promoted in recent years.

Supporting the individual learner

If you can get all or even some of your class using multimedia, this will allow you to give more individualised attention where needed while knowing that other learners have tasks to be getting on with. Learners who have been absent can use multimedia to catch up on missed classes if computers are available for individual study in a library or self-access centre.

INFO TECH

Multimedia in language learning

WHERE NEXT?

This book is for teachers who want to get a clearer understanding of what multimedia has to offer. We will explore the diversity of multimedia language learning materials available and suggest ways in which you can exploit it. We will also consider how multimedia can be used to support learning in and out of class, and how it can be integrated into an existing curriculum or used to provide supplementary activities. The ground covered will be useful irrespective of how much hardware and software your school currently has available.

The introduction of multimedia materials into a language learning programme will be most effective if there is a clear rationale for its use. This rationale should be driven by the methodology already underlying the design of the curriculum. A number of key questions will need attention as a rationale is considered. If multimedia is to be used:

- what should the balance be between the use of the technology and other activities?

5

- will the role of the course book change?

- will the roles of the teacher and learner undergo any change?

Experimenting with multimedia will provide you with the type of experience which will help to answer these questions.

2 | Understanding multimedia

THE FEATURES OF MULTIMEDIA

Multimedia is of educational value not simply because it enables the presentation of information in a variety of media, but also because of the way it allows that information to be accessed. We are used to information being presented in a linear way, so we expect a book to be laid out in a coherent and logical structure which flows from the beginning to the end. Multimedia allows information to be presented in a different way. It can be divided into chunks which may be read, viewed or listened to in any sequence chosen by the user. The user does this by jumping, or navigating, from one screen of information to another by clicking with the mouse on buttons, **hotwords** or **hotspots** which provide links to related information. This non-linear, associative way of arranging information is called **hypermedia**. Although this idea sounds complex, in practice it is simple to use and is now commonplace in computer applications. It will already be familiar to you if you have used the World Wide Web.

Hypermedia is important because it brings some of the interactive elements necessary for effective computer-based teaching and learning materials. It is hypermedia which gives teachers or learners control over the path they choose through the materials. In language learning materials it can provide instant access to mono-lingual or bilingual dictionary entries, glossaries, transcriptions, translations, examples of correct pronunciation, grammar explanations, visual support, and cultural background information. Hypermedia also plays a part in providing feedback to learners in the course of doing exercises.

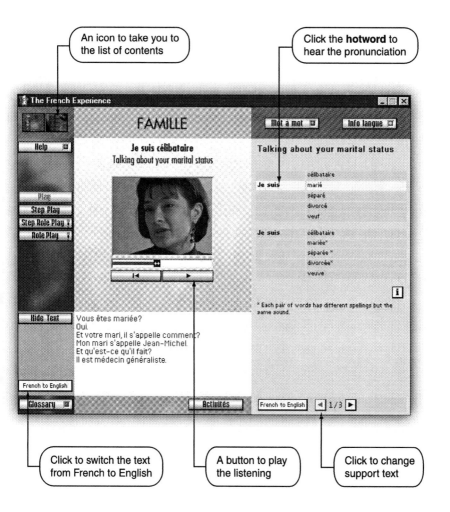

A sample screen from a multimedia language learning package
The French experience (© BBC Worldwide Ltd)

Multimedia in language learning

WHERE AND WHEN MULTIMEDIA CAN BE USED

Irrespective of the language skill or communicative competence being developed, the language learning process can be divided into four essential stages. These are:

- presentation of the new material or language element to be learnt;

- work familiarising the student with this material to support understanding and memorisation;

- a communicative exchange in which the new language is used productively; and finally

- a reflective period in which work on the new language element is consolidated by applying the language in different contexts such as a writing exercise.

This final stage is likely to involve attention to form and accuracy involving some type of questioning and written practice.

Given the normal lesson length, working through all four stages in a class period is impractical. The stages can be spread across lesson periods and involve homework. Multimedia can support all these stages and provide work in and out of class. However, the degree to which it can be exploited will depend on the available resources.

Presentation

Experienced teachers accumulate routines and materials (such as pictures, audio clips, diagrams, video clips) to help contextualise the presentation of new language. Gathering and storing resources is time and space consuming. A lot of these resources can be turned into digital versions (digitised) to be stored more efficiently on a computer. For example, pictures collected to present vocabulary for food items can be scanned and turned into digital pictures for viewing on a computer screen or printing out on a worksheet. Alternatively, it will be easier to take the images of food you need from one of the many cheap digital libraries of pictures available on CD-ROM. The cheapest and most widely available libraries usually originate from North America and the images tend to be either culturally neutral or have an American bias. Using digitised teaching content materials simplifies the storage, organisation, transportation,

8

distribution and presentation of these materials. How the materials are used with the class will depend on the equipment available.

Computer-based presentation

A good computer-based presentation can be highly effective as you are able to arrange the sequencing of the presentation, and to build in colour, sound and images. Access to a computer, video projector and whiteboard enables a presentation to be viewed by the whole class. A front of class presentation, and the whole class teaching it supports, has clear benefits during certain stages of a lesson. The powerful visual nature of a presentation will hold the learners' attention and allow you to focus concentration on the language items being covered. Time need not be wasted cleaning boards and writing up the information the learners need. You are also able to monitor the learners' reactions to and understanding of new input by putting questions to the class.

If a cluster of machines is available or a computer lab or pool, then the presentation materials can be viewed by pupils at their own pace. Once you have used a digital presentation, it is clear where it needs improvement ready for use with the next class. Even early efforts at producing presentations can result in useful materials if you follow a few basic principles (see Chapter 5).

9

You do not necessarily have to prepare your own multimedia material for the presentation section of the lesson. The multimedia resources that the school has bought should have sections which cover the language area you intend to present. When you have found this material, you will have to choose whether or not to project it in a whole class activity or have learners working at computers individually, in pairs or small groups.

Familiarisation

This is the 'practice' stage of the language learning process – as in the classic 'Presentation, Practice, Production' (PPP) lesson staging. Learners need to work on understanding and memorising the new language elements so that they can integrate them with what they already know. Familiarisation can be achieved through an assortment of tasks which emphasise the meaning of the new language.

Some computer-based language learning materials have been criticised for being remorselessly drill like. However, repetitive activities do help learning in the familiarisation stage provided they do not bore learners. With multimedia the learner's interest is held for a number of reasons:

- the majority of activities take place in a stimulating and vivid environment over which the learner has control;

- the same language elements can be recycled through a gamut of different computer-based exercises;

- learners can access a range of instant help facilities to assist them to complete tasks;

- good multimedia provides appropriate feedback which is designed to extend learners' knowledge when they are correct and to assist them when wrong.

If you have to cope with mixed-ability classes, you will appreciate the flexibility of many packages which allow individual learners to work at their own pace and level.

10

Communication

At this important stage you face the challenge of creating an appropriate communicative context in which learners can use the newly learned language in a genuinely communicative exchange. Although computers and multimedia can facilitate the communication stage in a number of ways, it is important to stress what computers cannot do. Computers and the programs they run cannot converse with people. Some programs can simulate a limited conversation and may in future offer language learning potential. Other programs allow you to turn speech to text or text to speech, or let you control simple functions like opening and saving files on your computer. However, none of these programs offers the type of flexibility of response that is a feature of human communication.

Multimedia language learning packages are available which offer interesting and intriguing simulations, generally making the learner a participant in a story or adventure played out on the screen. As the simulation progresses learners experience a range of situations resulting from choices they have made. They may for example find themselves in a railway station, hotel lobby, restaurant or police station where they communicate with on-screen characters. However, this communication is limited to choosing from a selection of prepared responses.

These choices have consequences for the learner such as getting something to eat or landing in jail. Although some simulations vividly contextualise language and give useful listening and reading practice, they cannot simulate the diversity of real communication.

While on-screen simulation activities have a place, it is the potential of multimedia to stimulate, support and sustain real communication between learners which is more valuable. Multimedia can prepare learners for a variety of communicative exchanges which take place either at the computer or away from it. The ideas, language and other elements needed for a communication activity can all be presented and rehearsed through multimedia. At all levels multimedia resources can be used as a source of material for information gap activities or as a foundation for role plays. At higher levels information presented in a multimedia format can be used to sustain simulations or projects spanning several lessons.

One of the most fruitful roles for multimedia in the communication stage is using the computer as a medium of communication between groups of language learners in different schools. E-mail is now being used locally, nationally and internationally to link groups learning the same target language or those learning each other's languages. A range of approaches can be taken to the structuring of these exchanges, but whatever work takes place all types of media can be used. E-mail allows pupils to send photographs, pictures, sound files, or electronic presentations to their partner group, so this is far from a text-only facility. To avoid sending large files via e-mail, all these resources can be included in pages put up on the World Wide Web. For more insights into how to make this use of computers communicatively orientated in this way see InfoTech 1 *E-mail: Using electronic communications in foreign language teaching* by Kate Townsend and InfoTech 3, *WWW The Internet* by Terry Atkinson.

11

Consolidation

This stage involves activities which encourage learners to reflect on what they have studied and apply it in new contexts. This consolidation has generally been achieved through written activities with greater attention being given to form and accuracy than at the communicative stage. Any of the standard computer applications, such as word processors, which now offer multimedia facilities can be used to support reflection. Learners can, for example, produce a multimedia

record of what they have learned ready for your assessment. The big language learning multimedia publishers are now producing a new generation of materials which are less concerned with replicating the teacher but instead put useful tools in learners' hands. For example, packages are now available which support learners who are working on second language writing tasks.

PLANNING AND ORGANISATION – PRACTICAL CONSIDERATIONS

Given the potential that multimedia has to support language learning, what key practical aspects of multimedia use need to be considered before you are able to exploit it? The take-up of multimedia will be determined by two major issues. The first is how extensively multimedia will be integrated into the language learning curriculum. This decision is bound to be linked to other uses of computers in the language learning process, for example the Internet, and to the general scale of computer use in your school. The second major issue is resourcing, which will include a whole range of decisions concerning hardware, software, staffing and training and support issues, all of which ultimately come to down to finances.

12

Hardware

Careful planning of hardware provision is a key factor in the successful exploitation of computer technology, increasingly talked about as Information and Communications Technologies (ICT), in schools. Decisions related to hardware will almost certainly be taken at school or even local education authority level. At whatever level these decisions are taken, language teachers or heads of language departments should make their views known, because the type of machines that are bought, how they are distributed and the type of networked support they have will have a major impact on their use in the language learning curriculum.

For you to be able to use multimedia, your school will need to invest in multimedia computers. These will come with a sound card fitted, allowing sound to be both played and recorded if a headset and microphone are plugged into the computer. Fortunately these peripherals can now be bought as relatively cheap, combined units. Unfortunately this equipment is vulnerable to

damage and theft, and some schools now insist that learners provide their own headsets.

The multimedia computer will also come with a DVD or CD-ROM drive, unless the school is investing in a more elaborate system which allows multimedia to be accessed through a local network linking all the computers. This will mean the multimedia can be accessed from a central computer called a server. Distribution of the computers within the school also needs careful consideration and it is important that teachers are consulted at this stage to decide how, where and when they want to make use of computers.

Perhaps the most significant problem that language departments face in hardware terms is the over-concentration of resources applied to this area. Hardware is just one area of expenditure, but it always has the largest proportion of the available budget spent on it. Often this leaves other key areas under-resourced. It is these areas we now turn to.

Software

13

The software budget will need to cover the purchase of multimedia language learning packages and other learning related items such as foreign language dictionaries for word processors. The size of the budget will again relate to the position that multimedia is to take in the curriculum. Materials may form the core of a course or simply be used as a supplement. Bear in mind which element of the process of language learning the multimedia materials are intended to support and whether they are for use in or out of class time. A framework for evaluating multimedia language learning packages is included in Chapter 3.

Staffing and training

Hardware and software alone are not enough to promote successful language learning. You, as the teacher, must be able to use the technology with some degree of confidence. This requires a carefully managed program of ICT training designed to give you the skills you need to make the best use of the technology. This demands an investment of time and money, and with the rapid pace of ICT development, this training will need regular updating throughout your teaching career.

ICT training needs to be subject specific if multimedia is to be used successfully. Ideally this will involve you seeing convincing examples of how other teachers are using computer applications in their everyday teaching of languages. If this includes good examples of multimedia use, then this should provide you with a model which you can apply to your own teaching situation. Having started to use the technology, you can then go on to develop and implement your own approach.

Fortunately ICT training for teachers has improved in recent years. In the United Kingdom this has been helped by the *New Opportunities Fund* (NOF) which has allocated National Lottery money to fund in-service teacher training. Courses designed to show you how the new technologies can be integrated into your subject area are now available throughout the UK. Several major educational organisations, such as CILT, the Open University, and Learning and Teaching Scotland, are involved in running courses. To make the training as widely available as possible some courses, or elements of courses, are being delivered on-line. For more on what the *New Opportunities Fund* is doing in the education field see the NOF Website (address in Chapter 6).

14

Technical support

Teachers with good ICT skills will use multimedia if it is available and appropriate, but even these teachers will not use facilities which have not been properly set up or are regularly unavailable because of breakdowns. Computers and software are not yet as robust or dependable as teachers would like them to be. This is especially true when computing resources are being used by a large number of users. Budgeting for good technical support to maintain equipment is therefore vital.

Support is also needed for simple but important elements of multimedia use. This will include things like: cataloguing materials; maintaining records of materials; keeping teachers up to date with what is available; booking in and out CD-ROMs, headphones or speakers, support materials, etc to teachers or pupils. These are departmental rather than institutional responsibilities.

GETTING STARTED

The introduction of multimedia into the language learning curriculum will be more successful if you can answer the following questions for your school:

INFO TeCH

Multimedia in language learning

- Why is the technology being introduced?

- How will its use integrate with the existing approaches and goals in the curriculum?

- Will the curriculum be altered to match the materials chosen or materials chosen to match the curriculum?

- Who will benefit and how?

- Will multimedia be used alongside other information and communications technologies?

- If it will, what other ICTs will be used, when, where and how?

- How much can be spent?

InfoTech 5 *Putting achievement first: Managing and leading ICT in the MFL department* by David Buckland raises additional questions that need to be tackled when managing the integration of ICT and MFL.

15

Schools will benefit from a carefully staged introduction of the technology. Starting small has a number of benefits as mistakes made on a small scale will have less impact on learners and waste less time and money than a large scale project. As you experiment, the results should be monitored so that you can then redirect the use of multimedia in response to successes and failures.

In order to avoid introducing technology for technology's sake, identify a weak area of the curriculum and try to improve the delivery of that area with multimedia materials. At this early stage the materials used should be taken from something which is commercially available.

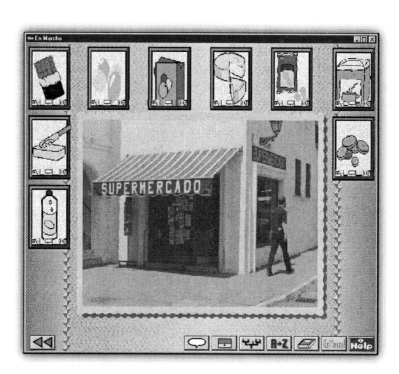

16

A visit to the supermarket
¡En marcha! (© Granada Learning Ltd)

The type of activity you could usefully experiment with is the presentation of vocabulary items using a CD-ROM. The illustration above is taken from *¡En marcha!* (Granada Learning). Among other things, the disk covers over a thousand Spanish words for learners at lower levels. Here the vocabulary being presented is connected to a visit to the supermarket. Pictures of the lexical items to be learnt are shown, the words are pronounced in isolation and in a sentence. Translations are also available. The simple controls allow whoever is using the package to decide whether to listen to the language, or read it, or both. The user can also hide or show the pictures illustrating the vocabulary items. This format would be effective for the presentation of new vocabulary items and for reviewing them. The activities could be used for whole class work, if you have the equipment for projecting the screen at the front of class, or for individual or pair work if a computer room or self access centre with computers is available.

INFO TECH

Multimedia in language learning

If initial experiments into using multimedia prove successful, then further work can be carried out with the same material to see how effective it is in servicing other areas of the curriculum. As you begin to work with multimedia materials you will quickly discover what works with your learners and what does not. This then allows you to make more informed and useful evaluations of multimedia materials.

A variety of advice and guidance to help you in your initial forays into multimedia can be found on World Wide Web sites. These include the British Educational Communications and Technology Agency (BECTA) site, the Virtual Teachers Centre, the National Grid for Learning and the CILT Website. Website addresses for all these are available in Chapter 6.

SUCCESS

As indicated above, the successful introduction of multimedia into the curriculum depends more on you, as the teacher, than any other factor. You will face the challenge of working with new technologies and new media and linking their use into the curriculum. If you are to achieve this, you need support, training, encouragement and some tangible reward for the effort you will need to put in.

17

THE FUTURE

The future for multimedia in the educational field is increasingly bright. The cost of both hardware and software is constantly falling, while the speed and reliability of both are rising. Where and when people can access multimedia is also changing as the boundaries between different technologies begin to disappear. Some users are now picking up their e-mails on their mobile phones while others surf the Web using their televisions. This process of convergence will give ICTs growing importance in all areas of education.

Two major technologies which are developing at breakneck speed and which will have a growing effect on multimedia use in the languages field, are the Web and DVD. The potential for fully featured multimedia over electronic networks is already with us. However, its general availability is limited by the low

capacity of many of the existing network connections into homes and schools. As these improve the potential for on-line learning will begin to be realised more widely. The BBC is already demonstrating some of what can be done on its educational Websites (see Chapter 6 for website addresses). Publishers are also supporting the multimedia materials they provide on CD-ROM with additional updated materials accessed over the Web, and on-line support from teachers via e-mail. In the languages field this is being taken to its logical conclusion by the company Vektor which is offering A level courses in French, German and Spanish through multimedia learning materials on CD-ROM, and study support and conversation practice with a teacher via video conferencing.

18

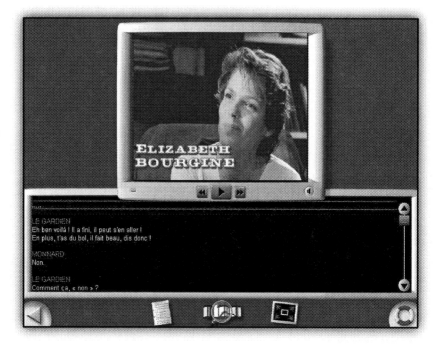

One of the new generation of DVD-ROMs for language learning
Advanced French – Interactive video language learning with 'Au cœur de la loi'
(© Eurotalk Interactive)

Multimedia in language learning

DVD technology makes it possible to store huge quantities of digital information on a disk the size of a CD-ROM. These disks are intended for viewing on a television monitor connected to a DVD player, but can also be viewed on a computer which has a DVD drive. Over the next few years films on DVD will steadily replace films on video tape. This will bring a number of benefits to language teaching as DVDs offer the capacity to switch subtitles on and off and, depending on the disk, to switch between a range of languages in both text and audio. You will be able to play sections of target language films or purpose-made language learning materials with or without transcriptions on screen. DVD-ROMs, which must be played on a computer, take this concept further. Like DVDs, these allow you to view video images which can be supported with the usual range of learning and support materials that multimedia provides. Given the enthusiasm of teachers and learners for video, it is likely that DVD-ROMs will offer considerable benefits to learners, provided that high quality learning materials are developed to support the video. Language learning DVD-ROMs are already available for French, Italian, Spanish, German and Greek.

19

Any explorations you make in the multimedia area will help prepare you for a future in which this technology is set to play a greater part in language learning.

3 Dedicated multimedia for language learning

Over recent years a steady stream of language learning multimedia materials have been published. Most of these have been CD-ROM packages intended as complete courses designed for learners working on their own. There is a concentration of materials for beginner, elementary and lower intermediate levels (e.g. *¡En marcha!*, *Directions 2000*, *Breakthrough French*) with a noticeable lack for higher levels. The cost and quality of these packages vary considerably, which means that careful evaluation of a product before buying it is essential.

CATEGORIES OF MATERIAL

The bulk of language learning multimedia materials fit into one of the following categories:

Complete language learning courseware

In essence these programs are teach-yourself courses which try to replicate as many of the functions of a teacher as can be programmed in. Generally, each unit is structured around a functional or thematic aspect of the target language presented in a situational context. Exercises and tasks on vocabulary, grammar and skills areas are provided so learners can practise and memorise new language. As learners work through tasks, appropriate feedback is given. *Breakthrough French interactive* (Palgrave) is a good example of this type of disk, as are the *Expressions* disks (Vektor) for French, German, Spanish, and Italian.

Reference materials

Although a number of bilingual electronic dictionaries are now available, most of these are not specifically designed for language learning. They are predominantly textual, for example the *Oxford Hachette French dictionary* (Oxford University Press), with little made of the multimedia potential. Others, such as the *Multi-lingual talking picture dictionary* (Softkey) use both pictures and sound. All are fast and versatile, and particularly valuable when learners are writing or working on vocabulary activities. Suggestions on how electronic dictionaries can be exploited are given in Chapter 4.

In addition, most dedicated language learning CD-ROMs provide either a glossary or an abridged dictionary. For example, *The French reference* (Language Intelligence) offers an electronic dictionary which includes all GCSE French syllabus vocabulary. As well as reading definitions learners are able to hear the pronunciation of many of the words.

Exam preparation, assessment and testing

21

Some packages have been designed to prepare pupils for national exams, these provide a range of revision practice appropriate to the relevant syllabus, for example *GCSE French, GCSE German, GCSE Spanish* (Europress), *Revise GCSE French* (Libra Multimedia), and *GCSE French* (Dorling Kindersley). The design of the material on these disks and the activities and feedback are similar to the courseware packages described above. Despite the interest in computer-based assessment very little multimedia for assessment purposes is available.

Simulations

Simulations present learners with one central challenge, such as solving a mystery. A popular example of this genre is *Who is Oscar Lake?* (Language Publications Interactive) which is available for French, Spanish and German. To complete the simulation successfully, learners have to work through a series of micro tasks, most of which are essentially listening or reading activities. Although the computer game-like environment of simulations is frequently alienating to adults, for those younger learners who are used to computer games it can be appealing and motivating. The better simulations convey some of the cultural background to the target language. (For more on simulations see Chapters 2 and 4.)

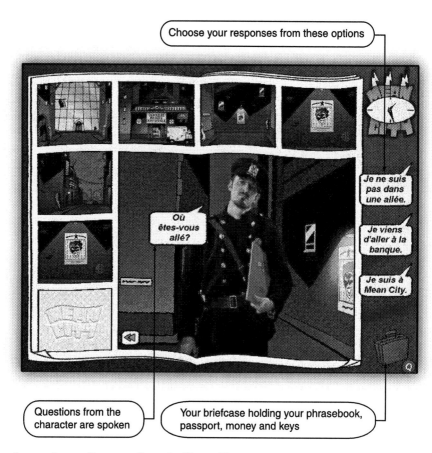

Choose your responses from these options

Je ne suis pas dans une allée.

Je viens d'aller à la banque.

Je suis à Mean City.

Où êtes-vous allé?

Questions from the character are spoken

Your briefcase holding your phrasebook, passport, money and keys

22

Answering police questions in *Mean City*
Mean City – learn French and survive (© DK Interactive Learning – Language Arts)

Tools

One category of multimedia materials offering the greatest potential for language learning is that of 'tools'. With these applications the materials designers have worked on the principle that computers are not teaching machines but tools which help people to get things done. A word processor is essentially an elaborate and powerful replacement for a pen; if the word

processor has a spell checker and fonts appropriate for the target language, then writing that language is supported. Taking this idea one step further, publishers have designed multimedia packages which act as a resource and inspiration for pupils learning to write in a second language. *Writers' workshop* and *Young writers' workshop* (Granada Learning) provide useful materials and activities for learners writing in French, German or Spanish.

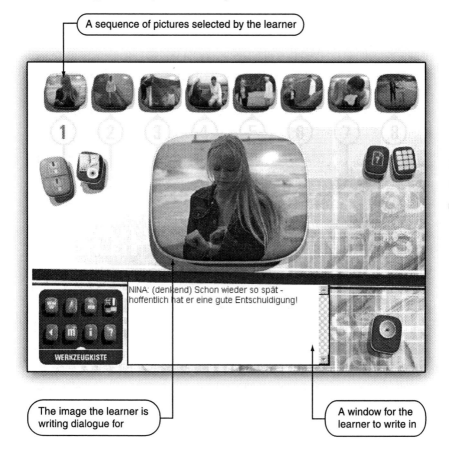

A sequence of pictures selected by the learner

NINA: (denkend) Schon wieder so spät - hoffentlich hat er eine gute Entschuldigung!

WERKZEUGKISTE

23

The image the learner is writing dialogue for

A window for the learner to write in

A photo story scene designed to help learners overcome writer's block
Writers' workshop (© Granada Learning Ltd)

Other applications which fall into the tool category include **concordancers** and **translation packages**, but these are essentially text based and do not exploit the potential of multimedia.

Special interest

This category includes multimedia materials designed for learners in the business area, those learning for special purposes, e.g. work or academic study, and children. Multimedia materials for MFL in these categories are available, but locating them can be challenging. Examples include: *Español de negocios* (Difusion) for business Spanish. Try searching on the Web or look in the ReCall Software Guide for specialist distributors (support information is given in Chapter 6).

24

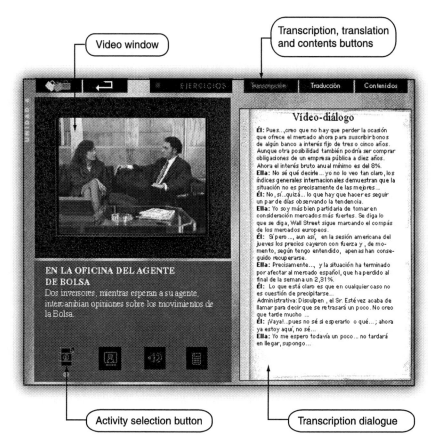

Multimedia to help improve your business negotiating skills in Spanish
Español de negocios (© Diffusion)

THE FOUR SKILLS, GRAMMAR AND VOCABULARY

Communicative language instruction has encouraged a functional approach to language learning which develops learners' competencies in the areas of listening, speaking, reading and writing. Although these distinctions are somewhat artificial because work on one skill frequently involves some degree of work in another, these categories are useful when designing a balanced syllabus and are used here to suggest ways in which interactive multimedia can support language study.

Listening

Multimedia can support the presentation, familiarisation and consolidation stages of listening work on a chosen language element. If computer projection equipment is available, you can select an audio clip from a CD-ROM and present this for whole class work. With well designed materials all the images, questions, answers, transcripts and the audio clip itself will be available. This approach is worth experimenting with, but multimedia materials will often achieve most if their unique combination of features can be accessed by an individual, pairs or small groups of learners working directly with the package. This allows learners to select from a range of listening activities in a series of structured exercises and tasks supported with rapid feedback and supplemented with other resources and on-line help.

The type of searching and rewinding which is integral to the use of a taped clip, whether just audio or video, is not necessary with multimedia clips. These can be accessed immediately with a button click and paused and replayed with fine degrees of control. Learners are able to choose whether to listen to materials with or without transcripts, and to access videos with or without sound. They can control the selection of activities and work through these at their own pace, repeating them if they find it beneficial. It is this tight integration of activities and resources, plus the control and interactivity, which makes multimedia so effective.

At each stage of the listening activity, including post-listening, a wide variety of tasks can be provided. These can include gap completion, word or sentence reordering, text and picture matching, and true/false and multiple choice questions. These are all familiar task types, but the multimedia format is used to present them in inventive and interactive formats which help to maintain the learner's interest, recycle language and reinforce learning.

26

A listening activity based on video
Unterwegs (© Granada Learning Ltd)

The illustration above shows a simple listening activity based around a video clip from the CD-ROM *Unterwegs*. Having played the video, which can be seen top-left, the learner completes the multiple choice questions. Users can return to the video and replay it before choosing the correct answer, if they wish. They can also view the video text and hear the question and the correct answer read out. Feedback is aural. This is just one of several interlinked activities which are designed to develop the learner's vocabulary and the associated grammatical structures, used in German for talking about family members.

Speaking

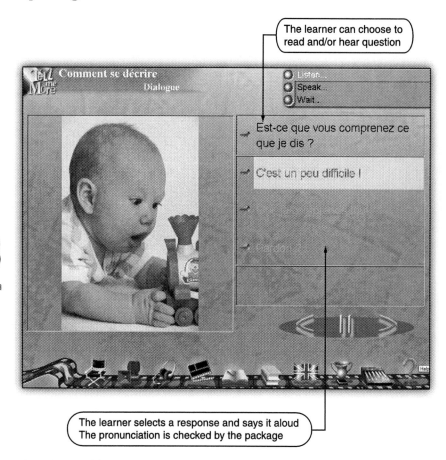

The learner can choose to read and/or hear question

The learner selects a response and says it aloud
The pronunciation is checked by the package

A package which promotes speaking and checks pronunciation
Tell me more PRO – Français (© Auralog)

Multimedia now provides support for work on speaking skills. The approaches used are similar to those found in language laboratories. At lower levels this involves dialogue builds in which the program acts as the learner's partner in an exchange. In most cases the computer does not provide feedback on performance. Instead, learners can compare their recordings with a pre-recorded

Multimedia in language learning

model. With suitable multimedia facilities learners can work on low level speaking activities in greater privacy than is possible in class. This helps them develop the ability to monitor their own language production. You can also use the recordings to assess the learners' performances and then give targeted, individualised feedback. By providing learners with appropriate monitoring strategies, they will be better able to evaluate and improve their own performance. The *Encounters* CD-ROMs available in French, German, Italian, Spanish and Portuguese (Hodder and Stoughton Educational), and *Essentials* available in French, German, Spanish and Italian (Vektor) include these types of activities.

Some multimedia programs help learners improve their intonation and pronunciation. These packages evaluate short recordings that the users make of single words, phrases or short sentences in the target language. This evaluation is achieved by comparing the learner's output with a pre-recorded model version. Performance can be compared with the model simply by listening or by looking at a graphical representation of the two recordings and comparing them. Given that many young learners are notoriously disinclined to produce anything resembling a 'foreign' accent, disks of this kind should not be dismissed lightly as the challenge they present is highly motivating.

29

Higher levels disks are now available which support learners in more demanding speaking activities such as recording a voice-over for a video clip of a news item, for example *Tele con textos, TV und Texte, Télé-textes* (Oxford University Press). Once again the control that the multimedia environment offers supports this type of sophisticated task-based activity.

Any multimedia package which incorporates the facility for learners to record their performance raises issues that you need to be aware of. Accessing sound on computers is straightforward, but recording sound can prove more challenging. Sound levels have to be set and hard disk space allocated on the computer for the recordings. These are relatively simple issues to deal with, but they are also aspects of the computer's set-up which other users may interfere with. On a more basic level you need to make sure that speakers, headphones and microphones are available and working.

Reading

When using some multimedia materials, the learner will have to read material in the target language simply to work through the activities. On-line support is constantly available to provide help with vocabulary, grammar, pronunciation or cultural issues as and when the reader runs into difficulties. Multimedia can also use a range of resources, such as background noises, photos, video clips, etc, to contextualise the situation that the text relates to. A number of packages are available which are either designed specifically to help learners develop their reading skills, for example *Autolire* (Collins Educational), or which are particularly suitable for reluctant readers.

A package with reading and listening potential
Impara l'Italiano con il figlio di Astérix (© Eurotalk Interactive)

Writing

Multimedia has a lot to offer the learner working on writing. At lower levels language consolidation through written work usually involves sentence completion activities, filling in gaps or tables, answering questions, making lists, word order or spelling tests, etc. Whilst learners are not required to compose complete sentences in these activities, they are required to work in the target language character set, and to develop awareness of syntax and the spelling rules of the language. This type of short writing exercise is ideally suited to familiarisation work in a multimedia format. Learners can type in their responses to given tasks and get rapid feedback.

Where text creation is concerned, multimedia cannot evaluate the language used but can support some of the areas which make up the writing process. Packages are available which prompt the writer through the early stages of writing such as brainstorming and ideas gathering. This can be done with pictures or videos which help learners to get over the blank page syndrome. Granada Learning's *Writers' workshop* (suitable for 11 to 16 year-olds) and *Young writer's workshop* (for lower ability 11 to 14 year-olds) are examples of this type of package. Some writing packages provide sample texts which show the learners typical features of the writing genre they are working on. An example of a package which does this is *Español escrito en ámbitos laborales* (Difusion). This is aimed at technical writers at intermediate and advanced levels who are writing in Spanish.

31

Grammar

Many multimedia language learning materials build in coverage of the target language grammar. The presentation of new grammar elements can be carefully structured and staged using suitable chunks of language presented sequentially. The presentation can avoid clutter by revealing and hiding language or information on screen as necessary. Colour and animation are used for emphasis and sound support for pronunciation features. Learners can stop the presentation, go back and repeat stages as necessary. Following the presentation a range of activities can be used to familiarise the learner with the new language. Rapid feedback means that even mundane and repetitive activities can be motivating in an interactive environment. The BBC's *The French experience* demonstrates how effectively this can be achieved. An even tighter grammar focus is provided in Granada Learning's *French grammar studio* which is helpful for GCSE preparation. While it is completely text based, the *GramEx* series (Hodder and Stoughton Educational) for French, German, Spanish, Italian, and English is also useful.

Vocabulary

Using pictures to present and practise items of vocabulary is not new to teachers, but the speed and efficiency with which pictures can be accessed using multimedia will be for many. Multimedia has the potential to present new vocabulary with a supporting image for clarification, while showing how the word is spelt, and how it is pronounced both in isolation and in a phrase. Familiarisation work can be given with picture and word matching, gapfills for spelling, etc. The speed and ease of access to interactive dictionaries and glossaries, using one click hyperlinks and cross-referencing, encourages even the less inspired learner to look up unknown words. Some packages keep a record of the vocabulary that the learner has looked at while using the package. This can be printed out at any stage. The following CD-ROMs all have a major vocabulary element: *Talk now* (Eurotalk interactive) designed for beginners and available for 49 different languages, *World talk* (Eurotalk interactive) for intermediate level, currently available for 13 languages, *Language labs 2000* (Europress) available in French, German, Spanish and Italian.

32

EVALUATION

The cost and quality of purpose-made language learning materials vary considerably which makes a sound evaluation procedure essential when buying multimedia materials.

Basics

Purchasing decisions should not be based simply on promotional materials, catalogue descriptions or reviews. For a really worthwhile evaluation you need to request an inspection copy of the materials you are interested in from one of the materials distributors or publishers (see Chapter 6). Because initial impressions with multimedia can be misleading, it is important to familiarise yourself with the package you are evaluating. Features which seem attractive when you first use a disk (bright colours, big pictures, sound effects) can become

irritating, whereas materials which seem subdued and unappealing show their worth with more prolonged use. Ideally the views of both teachers and learners should be used in this evaluation process. You will find suggested evaluation criteria listed below.

Evaluation criteria

Technical considerations with CD-ROMs

Most technical issues related to multimedia use will be the responsibility of a technician, but it is useful to have some idea of the issues that need to be considered.

- **Instructions**: Check clear, concise technical instructions are provided.

- **Installation**: CD-ROMs need to be 'installed' on a computer before they can be used. This procedure allows the disk to be run, and provides an icon to start the package. Installation should be quick and straightforward.

- **Networkable software**: If your school uses a network, then installing and running software may prove more simple and faster than if the computers are standalone. However, if packages are to be run on a network, then they must be networkable and a network licensing agreement paid for.

The multimedia design

As you evaluate a multimedia package, consider what it offers in comparison with a book and a tape.

- **Navigation**: Is it clear what is on the disk? Can you get to the material you want to use? Do you know where you are when you are using the materials? Is it easy to move backwards and forwards? Do you get lost?

- **Aesthetics**: Is the layout, colour and design of the materials attractive? Are they too dull or too garish?

- **Presentation**: How large is the window in which the package runs? Are the text and images clearly visible?

- **Text**: Is the text easy to read?

- **Images**: Do images assist learning or are they a distraction?

33

Multimedia in language learning

- **Sound**: Is the quality good? Is its use beneficial? Is it irritating? Does the learner have control over the audio? Can the sound be switched off?

- **Video and animation**: Do these add to the learning experience? Is their use integrated? Does the learner have control over the video?

- **Integration**: Are all the different media well and purposefully integrated?

- **Interactivity**: This can be measured by the degree of control and flexibility available to learners using the package. This relates to four main areas: How often are learners offered choices? How many choices are they offered? What kind of choices are they offered? What significance does the learner's choice have? How involved does the learner feel with what is happening on screen? The learner may be given too much or too little choice leading to irritation or confusion.

- **Computer 'personality'**: Is the package attractive or alienating to use?

- **Tailorability**: How many aspects of the package can learners tailor to their preferences?

- **Help**: Is a comprehensible help facility readily available?

34

Pedagogical factors

The evaluation process should consider the pedagogical factors underpinning the design. Consider the following:

- **Educational aim**: What aspect/s of language learning is the package designed to support? How does it do this? Does it succeed?

- **Learning objectives**: Are these made clear to learners? Does the software facilitate their achievement?

- **The language learning approach**: Does the package use an approach to language learning that you recognise? Is this one which you believe is effective?

- **Integration**: Can the materials usefully support the existing syllabus? Is there a role and place for them for in or out-of-class use?

- **Support materials**: Are there support materials available which provide additional practice or extension work? Is the package itself designed to support a course book?

- **Interest**: Is the material sufficiently interesting that you and your learners will want to return to it?

- **Input**: Is the input language appropriate for the level of your learners? Is new language contextualised and its use meaningful?

- **Output**: What opportunities are there for learner output? Are these written or spoken?

- **Practice**: Is a range of learning activities provided? With each activity is it clear what the learner has to do? Are the activities interesting and challenging or repetitive and predictable? Do they match the language being learnt? Can learners continually get questions right by guessing?

- **Feedback**: Does the feedback support learning or does it simply tell learners when they are right and wrong and not why?

35

- **Accuracy**: Does the material contain factual, linguistic, or cultural mistakes?

- **Creativity**: Can learners manipulate, reconstruct and reuse material presented in the package?

- **Authorability**: Can teachers or pupils create new materials using the package?

- **Tracking**: Does the package keep a record of each user so they can return to their place when they reuse the software?

- **Assessment**: Does the package assess the learner's language level? If so, how accurate is this?

- **Offensive material**: Does the package contain material which some learners may find offensive?

- **Cultural issues**: Does the material present the culture in which the target language is spoken? Is this aspect presented sensitively or crudely?

These questions are not intended as a checklist but as prompts for consideration and discussion. The amount of effort put into the evaluation should be in proportion to the importance of the materials in the syllabus.

AVAILABILITY

The difficulty in actually obtaining multimedia materials has undoubtedly played a part in their slow adoption in education. A number of educational materials distribution companies now supply inspection copies of CD-ROMs. Some of these are listed in Chapter 6. These companies will be happy to provide you with a catalogue showing what is available. In addition, you can visit the BECTA website which has a section with reviews of CD-ROMs available for language teaching. In the United Kingdom the Comenius Centres and CILT libraries also have both the facilities and the materials to allow you to work through a wide range of packages. We hope this chapter will have whetted your appetite and you will take a look at some of the available materials and go on to experiment with them.

36

4 Exploiting authentic material on CD-ROM

Many teachers use authentic newspaper or magazine articles and recordings of television or radio programmes as a basis for activities to be worked on during lesson time or as homework. In this chapter some ways of exploiting authentic multimedia packages are considered. 'Authentic' is used here to refer to any material which is not specifically produced for language learning, but for native speakers either for education or entertainment.

THE ADVANTAGES OF USING AUTHENTIC MATERIALS

Authentic multimedia materials can offer a rich source of texts, diagrams, maps, explanations, video clips, short extracts of authentic speech, news articles, reviews, games and activities, all of which provide the learner with considerable exposure to the target language (spoken and written). Produced by major companies for the mass market of home users, these materials benefit from far greater levels of investment than educational materials, and yet remain relatively inexpensive. They can be purchased in computer stores and specialist shops and even many supermarkets (in the country of the target language), or through your usual supplier of foreign language books and educational materials. Designed for and by native speakers, they offer a genuine portrayal of the culture of the target language. Using authentic multimedia materials enables learners to develop useful transferable skills and presents possibilities for cross-curricular work.

POTENTIAL DRAWBACKS

Using authentic packages will involve you in the preparation of support materials, just as when choosing to use an authentic video, text or song to work on in class. This means that you must be prepared to spend time becoming familiar with the CD-ROM and preparing appropriate tasks for the learners. This is a simple process, and rewarding in the long term, but as practising teachers we are well aware of the existing heavy demands on our time. As in the preparation of tasks using other 'authentic' sources, it is important to remember that it is the task which should be designed to suit the level of the students, and not the text.

DIFFERENT TYPES OF AUTHENTIC MATERIALS

38

There is a wide range of authentic multimedia which can be exploited for use by language learners. In this section, some indications of the different types of authentic materials available, and some suggestions of how they can be used in the classroom at different levels, are presented. As you familiarise yourself with multimedia, you will begin to appreciate its potential and think of many ways you can use these materials.

Dictionaries

The multimedia format of mono- and bilingual dictionaries available on CD-ROM may be motivating for students and will liven up potentially uninspiring dictionary work as learners can quickly find their way around the dictionary. In addition to the information found in a standard dictionary, help may be given with the pronunciation of words which can be heard in isolation and sometimes within a sentence. Supporting visuals help comprehension and some dictionaries carry additional information about famous people, cities, sights, etc.

Effective but simply prepared work sheets such as word searches, classifying words, vocabulary sets or work on collocations can be produced or adapted from existing materials. Students can then keep a printed record of the work they have done and add this to their own bank of useful vocabulary.

1) Find the following words in your dictionary. Put them in the correct column. You can draw a picture next to the word, to help you remember the word.

2) Practise saying the words in each column. Listen carefully to the way each word is pronounced.

Les Légumes

| pomme de terre | chou | chou-fleur | concombre | carotte |
| navet | radis | oignon | laitue | poireau |

Masculine	Feminine
Un...	Une...

3) Now match the vegetable with a colour from this box.

39

rouge	blanc	blanche	vert	verte	orange

Example Un concombre vert

A vocabulary worksheet, suitable for use at Key Stage 3, to be used with a French multimedia dictionary

This activity is possible with any bilingual dictionary which provides aural pronunciation such as Softkey's *Multi-lingual talking picture dictionary*.

Reference works

This category includes both general encyclopaedias, such as *Encarta* (Microsoft), *Mon encyclopédie* (Micro Application), *Encyclopédie* (Hachette Mulitimédia), and a wide range of reference works which cover a more specific subject area, such as a period in history – *2000 ans d'histoire en France, Découvertes* (Havas Interactive), a country or its regions – *France merveilleuse* (Emme), *Villes en France* and *Voyage au Maroc* (Acta), a famous person's life – *Alexandre Dumas – Un aventurier de génie* (Acamédia) or an area such as cinema – *Cinémascope* (Canal +Multimédia) or nature – *Encyclopédie du corps*

INFOTECH

Multimedia in language learning

humain en 3D (Larousse) and *Encyclopédie de la nature* (Havas Interactive). It also encompasses what might be loosely termed 'How to' packages, which would include titles such as *Réussir son code de la route, CVs et lettres de motivation* (Micro), etc.

In addition to the wealth of information in text form and supporting photographs that can be found in encyclopaedias in book form, there are animations, video and audio clips, interactive activities and Internet links. The multimedia format motivates learners to look up information and undertake research in a way that books may fail to do. Learning to search for information is an important skill which actively engages the learners in the process of research and discovery, empowering them to make informed but personal choices about their studies.

Quizzes

40

Activities such as quizzes and matching games are often included in encyclopaedias (e.g. *Encarta* mind maze, *Mon encyclopédie* quiz) and other reference works. Because these materials are produced for native speakers, the content of the quizzes may be very culture-specific and challenging, but working in groups encourages discussion.

A quiz taken from a French multimedia encyclopaedia
Mon encyclopédie 1998 (All rights reserved Data Becker & Micro Application)

Multimedia in language learning

You can also produce your own quizzes to be used with these materials, bearing in mind the level of the learners and their interests. Instructions on how to initiate a search should be included for learners who are unfamiliar with these materials. Working on finding the answers to a quiz is challenging and motivating, involving students in scanning texts for relevant information, and requiring them to think about useful words to help them to focus their search. It also provides them with an important opportunity for comparison of their own culture with that of the target language country. Learners can even prepare their own quizzes for the rest of the class, involving them in research, reading and writing.

Depending on the level of the students, questions can be in English or the target language:

True/False questions in the target language
Écrivez la bonne réponse.

Charles de Gaulle était le roi de France. | Vrai | Faux

Louis IX est né à Poissy le 24 avril 1214 | Vrai | Faux

Gérard Depardieu a cinquante ans | Vrai | Faux

41

Open questions in the target language

Quelle est la hauteur de la tour Eiffel?

Quel âge a Gérard Depardieu?

Où se trouve Mont Blanc?

Teacher-produced questions for use with a French multimedia encyclopaedia

Project work

The use of reference disks is invaluable in any project which involves research. Interactive CD-ROMs give learners the opportunity to research their topics by accessing information in a multimedia format, scanning through pictures, videos and written texts as they navigate their way around the CD-ROM using hyperlinks and search tools to find the information they need. Even when

seemingly working off target, learners are exposed to the language which they must endeavour to understand in order to select or reject specific items for use in their research. Text and pictures can be copied and pasted into word processed documents, or printed out.

There are many possibilities for this type of project, such as:

- **Planning a holiday/trip**

  This can be done using an encyclopaedia or a disk about a particular region. Small groups of students can either work on different aspects of the trip (what they will visit/eat/how to get there) or prepare visits to different towns/areas, and may have to persuade the rest of the class that going to their destination would be the most enjoyable.

- **Preparing a presentation**

  At higher levels, students should be encouraged to prepare and give short presentations on a subject related to the target language culture. This may be a talk about a town/area of the country or a festival/custom/historical event, etc, for which multimedia packages provide important reference sources of authentic material.

- **Creating a poster/book**

  Students can copy and print pictures or diagrams which can be used to decorate a poster or book on a variety of subjects. Students should be encouraged to add their own headings, labels and texts.

- **Finding out about an aspect of the target language culture such as food or festivals**

  Both encyclopaedias and more specific reference discs offer access to a wide range of information about the target language culture, an important aspect of the language learning experience.

- **Preparing a news report or television programme**

  Students can research an historically significant event, such as the destruction of the Berlin wall, the storming of the Bastille, and prepare and present, or write up, a news report as if they had been there, or are reporting from the scene. Video clips or pictures can be used with their own texts and voiceovers.

42

Writing tasks

Work done using a multimedia encyclopaedia can be used as a basis for writing activities at all levels. These can range from basic copying or guided writing tasks to far more demanding activities, such as essays or letters. Examples may be:

- guided writing tasks (parallel texts/letters/postcards);

- descriptions and comparisons (of cities, cultures, famous monuments, places, people, customs);

- postcards or letters (from one of the places or events researched);

- newspaper or magazine articles;

- a diary of an historical event;

- note taking;

- dictation.

43

The following exercises were designed for use with Key Stage 3/4 learners working with *Encarta encyclopédie 2000* (Microsoft), but could be used with other encyclopaedias or reference works, and of course in any language. The towns which were chosen are presented in short, clear articles. Stronger classes (time permitting) could tackle larger cities such as Paris, Lyon and Marseille which are covered in greater detail.

Groups of three work together at a computer. Each group is assigned one town. They should go to the article on their town and take notes under the headings given. This can be done as a group activity, but each student should complete their own notes.

	Dieppe	Tours	Bordeaux
Géographie			
Population (en 1990)			
Économie			
Industries			
Produits agricoles			
Édifices et monuments			

INFOTECH

Multimedia in language learning

Having completed their notes, students change groups so that in each group there is one student from each 'town'. This presents the opportunity for various activities which include students describing their towns, explaining new vocabulary, making comparative sentences about the towns or using their information to complete the 'master' grid above.

Follow-up exercises may include writing:

- sentences comparing the towns;
- a letter or postcard from someone living in or visiting the town;
- a poster/brochure advertising the town;
- a short description of the town;
- a parallel description of the students' own town;
- a guided writing task such as the ones below.

44

Description of a town

Using your notes, complete this text, choosing the correct alternative for your town.

Copy the corrected text into your workbook.

Dieppe		sud-ouest		au bord de la	Loire.
Bordeaux	ville du	centre-ouest	de la France,	sur la	Manche.
Tours		nord-ouest			Garonne.

	le textile		les produits chimiques.
Ses activités comprennent	la construction navale	et	l'industrie alimentaire.
	le raffinage de pétrole		le traitement du bois.

	une station balnéaire		130	
La ville est	un port de commerce	avec une population de	35	mille habitants.
	une ville universitaire		213	

INFO TECH

Multimedia in language learning

A postcard

Using your notes, complete this postcard.

Copy the corrected text into your workbook.

Cher ....,

Je passe quelques jours chez des amis qui habitent ici à ....

La ville, qui est très .... , se trouve dans le .... de la

France. Hier nous avons visité .... et demain nous allons

.... Chouette!

....

Leah

45

Listening

Video and audio clips on multimedia CD-ROMs can be used as you would use videos or cassettes in the classroom. While the computer should not be seen as a replacement for the video player in the classroom, activities are not limited to whole class activities, and individual students have a greater level of control over the way they work on specific activities. For ideas on using video in general, see Info Tech 4, *Video in language learning* by Brian Hill.

The following exercise is for use with *Encarta 2000*. 'Pour un dictionnaire' is read as a poem, and the text appears as below. Using the encyclopaedia allows easy access to follow-up work on the poet Soupault on the same disk.

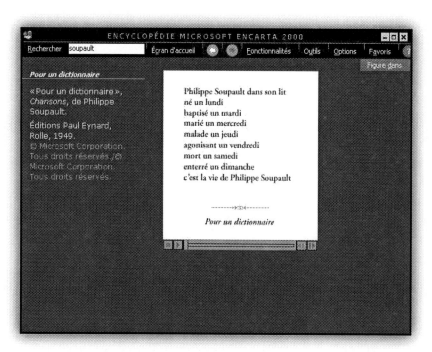

'Pour un dictionnaire' by Philippe Soupault
Encarta encyclopédie 2000 (© Microsoft). Screenshot reprinted by permission of Microsoft Corporation

Get students to listen to and read 'Pour un dictionnaire'. Working in pairs or small groups, they could:

■ mark off words they read/heard from the list below;

■ write down any words they remember;

mardi	mai	marié	un	nez
maladie	mort	malade	une	né

INFOTECH
Multimedia in language learning

- try to reconstruct the poem, the 'cards' below could be cut out and rearranged;

Philippe Soupault	dans son lit	né
un lundi	baptisé	un mardi
marié	un mercredi	malade
un jeudi	agonisant	un vendredi
mort	un samedi	enterré
un dimanche	c'est la vie de	Philippe Soupault

47

- take down the 'poem' as a dictation;
- translate the poem (and perhaps recognise its English equivalent).

Speaking

Texts, video and audio clips and animations provide material for:

- **Recording voiceovers**

  Students can prepare their own voiceovers for short video clips or to accompany diagrams or pictures. After listening to the text two or three times, and taking notes, they can reconstruct their own text, to be read out.

- **Descriptions and information exchange**

  Students can find out about different towns (or countries, important events in history, people, customs, etc) and describe what they have learnt. This may simply be a sentence or two, or a longer presentation depending on the level of the class.

Games

There are many multimedia games, such as detective games involving puzzle solving, e.g. *Versailles* (Cryo Interactive Entertainment), which learners will enjoy playing and which provide exposure to the target language. This language is often colloquial, which appeals to learners.

To make the most of their potential in the language learning process, it may be useful to think about using these materials as an alternative to the conventional Presentation, Practice, Production approach. Here the approach would be Prepare, Play and Produce. How long learners spend on each stage will depend on how you wish to exploit the material and on timetabling considerations.

Preparation can include an introduction to the concept of the game and its subject area, teaching the relevant vocabulary, and discussion of possible tactics. The next stage allows the learners to play the game. This may be best done in pairs or small groups and rules of play – use of the target language, agreement on moves, who has control of the mouse and keyboard – must be established.

48

The final stage involves learners in producing something as a follow-up activity. The choice of activity depends on the game played and the skill to be practised. Written tasks could be a report of the game, a witness' statement, an article or answering a prepared questionnaire relating to the game. Alternatively, learners can prepare a TV report of the crime or role play interviews or situations relating to the 'crime'.

Simulations

There are many excellent simulation games available. Although these are designed for use by native speakers, many have a high visual content and may be familiar to students in English and can therefore be used at more advanced levels. These are also best exploited using the 'PPP' stages as suggested for games but need to be thought of as long-term activities. Because of the similarity of approach, it will be helpful to look more closely at one example of this type of package and consider how it can be used in the language learning process.

For advanced level students, *SimCity 3000* (Electronic Arts) is available in English, French, German, Dutch and Swedish, all on a single CD-ROM. The

object of the simulation is to 'build' a new city, starting from scratch. This involves the players in a number of crucial decisions – how big should the city be, where should the school be built, how much water does the city need, what kind of transport system should be provided? Each decision has consequences – the more people who come to live in your city the greater the budget and the greater the need for facilities, placing the school outside the city requires adequate transportation, insufficient water supplies could lead to illness or social unrest. As the city builds up on the screen, players have to deal with the consequences of their decisions in order to move on to the next stage of development.

49

Consulting an advisor in *SimCity*™
SimCity 3000 (© 2000 Electronic Arts Inc.) All rights reserved.

The issues raised will call on work done in other disciplines such as geography, environmental studies, business studies or economics. These issues should be

Multimedia in language learning

raised and discussed in the preparation stage, allowing for pre-teaching of some vocabulary and preparing learners to make the most of the simulation.

Simply playing this simulation game provides an excellent basis for discussion and a great deal of exposure to the target language. Played in pairs or groups, learners must agree on each move they make, using the target language wherever possible. All information on the screen is in the target language and must be discussed and understood to make an informed decision. While learners are working on the simulation, it is a good idea for them to keep a record of new vocabulary they have learnt or want to ask questions about, and a record of the decisions they make and their consequences.

There are many possibilities for work following the simulation, which require students to speak and write in the target language. Learners could be asked to:

- write up an account of their experience;
- write a tourist leaflet or poster for the new town;
- write letters from citizens about issues raised (e.g. taxes, pollution);
- write an article about the new town for a newspaper;
- write letters to the town newspaper about a problem or a success;
- create a local newspaper;
- plan a visit to the town;
- make a video about the town or one of the issues raised;
- prepare and give election speeches;
- report on any riots/elections/building of new amenities.

The ideas in this chapter represent a sample of the possibilities for using authentic multimedia in the language classroom. If you are already familiar with preparing tasks and activities for your classes using texts, videos and recordings, then you will readily adapt to working with multimedia and appreciate the versatility and richness of its potential.

50

5

Teacher- and learner-produced multimedia materials

Some MFL teachers are already exploiting the multimedia potential of applications like word processors. They produce their own multimedia materials or get learners to produce multimedia work. In this chapter we consider how and why you might want to take on these challenges.

TEACHER-PRODUCED MULTIMEDIA MATERIALS

With good commercial multimedia materials already available and teachers short of the time and the skills needed to produce multimedia, why should you bother to produce your own multimedia? We believe there are persuasive reasons for doing so. Teachers already adapt course materials, prepare supplementary activities or, in inspired moments, produce something entirely new. Teachers produce materials because they interest and motivate learners, fill a gap in the existing materials, extend them or liven them up. The extra effort to produce materials comes from the ambition to teach as effectively and rewardingly as possibly. This is the same motivation that has driven some teachers to see what they can do with multimedia.

There are also good pedagogical reasons for you to produce materials. You are working closely with your learners and so know:

- what each group's needs are;

- where these needs are not being met by existing course materials;

- what works with each group;

- how to use time and materials to address the needs.

In essence you know how to teach and what works with the groups you teach. So any materials you produce should be more appropriate for your learners than those produced for mass consumption. In addition, learners respond positively to materials produced by their teacher, especially if these materials involve the learners in some way, either because they appear in them or because they played a part in producing them.

The ideas below illustrate ways in which teachers are already using the potential of multimedia as a supportive and creative tool to liven up or extend their teaching.

The word processor

The modern word processor allows the user to produce documents which in the past would have needed a desk top publishing package. This means you can produce your own worksheets, class magazines, or simulated menus, adverts, etc. The multimedia element in these materials is provided through the use of graphics and photos. If you can get learners viewing documents on a computer, then the multimedia potential really takes off. All graphics can be viewed in full colour, sound files can be included in documents and even digital video files can be played.

52

On-screen work sheets

With an on-screen worksheet you can include appropriate graphics for the area the learners are working on. These could be maps, photos, graphs, tables or illustrations. You can also add your own sound clips to documents. These can support text and images with pronunciation help, listening comprehension tasks or simple commentaries. Digital video and audio clips can also be added. Many of the resources you need will come with clip art libraries supplied with the word processor.

Preparing these worksheets will be time-consuming, but there are advantages. Once a document is prepared, it can be copied for use in a computer room, in a self access centre, or for learners to work with at home. The document can be saved and filed for reuse and then edited, adapted or updated as required. Once a successful model document or template has been created, this can be reworked to cover other areas of the syllabus. The learners gain because they get the

multimedia benefits plus the advantages of completing a worksheet at a computer, namely:

- clear, legible writing;

- the ability to edit their responses;

- possible access to fast L2 dictionaries and grammar checkers.

Teachers working in this way also comment on how much more motivated learners are when working on activities.

Sound annotations on learners' work

If you take in work as digital files, comments on the work can be made by adding text. In addition, with a microphone linked to your computer, sound clips can also be recorded and incorporated into a document. A small icon appears on the document at the point where you want the learner to be able to hear your feedback. By giving feedback on work in the target language, learners will be motivated to listen intensively. They will be able to listen to your comments as many times as they wish without asking you to repeat them. This will become increasingly important as more pupils get on-line at home.

53

Presentations

Presentation packages, such as *PowerPoint*, are being used increasingly in education. These easy-to-use packages enable you to present ideas and information using all the normal features of multimedia. When preparing a presentation, you create a series of screens. Each of these screens of material can be designed so that chunks of information are presented one after another. This gives you control over the staging of a lesson allowing you to reveal the language elements you want to present in a logical and progressive way. The presentation can be viewed in a number of ways:

- projected at the front of class;

- accessed by learners working individually at a computer;

- copied to disk and given out for self study;

- printed off and distributed on paper;

- put up on the Web for remote access;

Multimedia in language learning

- if the computer has the appropriate graphics card, it is also possible to connect a video recorder to it so that the presentation can be transferred to video tape and then viewed on a television.

This software allows you to prepare major aspects of the lesson ahead of time and to focus on the learners rather than writing up information on the board. It also gives you the potential to create materials with text, pictures, sound and animation which appeal to most learners and which may bring on board the more reluctant ones.

54

A screen from a presentation to teach German inflections
Animated German grammar (© Tim Jones, Braunton School and Community College)

The illustration above is taken from a presentation prepared by a teacher to teach German grammar in an entertaining and motivating way intended to appeal to the 'totally uninterested'. Viewed on screen, this presentation demonstrates the key features of an effective presentation:

- the amount of text on each screen is limited to bite sizes;

- text is large, clear and readable;

- colour is used to emphasise key language elements;

- animation, pictures and sound are used to attract attention and illustrate and highlight the grammatical features being covered;

- the screen layout has been carefully considered.

The potential range of uses for presentation software in language learning is vast:

- presenting new vocabulary using text and visuals;

- creating dialogue builds;

- building up grammar tables and question and answer forms;

- supporting listening exercises with contextualising visuals and key vocabulary;

- preparing learners for role plays;

- whole class work on reading comprehension, gap fills, etc.

55

Many activities currently done on the board would benefit from being presented in this way.

Computer-assisted language learning packages

A number of packages are available which are designed for the production of computer-based language learning activities. Applications in this category include *The authoring suite* (Wida), *Gapkit* (Camsoft), and *Hot potatoes* (Half-Baked Software). These types of applications now make much greater use of multimedia elements than they did in the past. If you are interested in this type of software, see InfoTech 2, *Text manipulation* by Sue Hewer.

Multimedia authoring packages

A number of powerful, yet easy to use authoring packages are now available including *HyperStudio* (Roger Wagner), *Junior multimedia lab* (Sherston*)*, *Illuminatus OPUS* (Digital Workshop) and *Mediator* (MatchWare). These packages are similar to presentation software but allow the user to do much

more. They give greater control over how the different media are laid out and incorporated into a finished product. They also offer more flexibility in how the information can be structured and accessed as they escape from the linear, book-like format of presentation software. This means information can be accessed in the same way as information on the Web through clicking buttons and hotwords. Using an authoring program, you can include gap fills, true/false and multiple-choice questions into the work you create. With a little training these authoring packages can be used to create impressive pieces of interactive multimedia. Language teachers are experimenting with authoring packages and produce work ranging from the simple to the highly sophisticated.

56

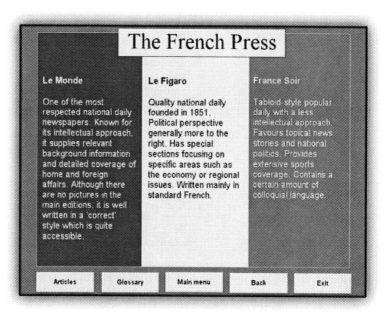

Screen from materials designed to accompany a text on the French press
(© Jane Carne, South Bank University, London)

The illustration above is taken from an application produced by a teacher to support learners studying a range of text taken from the French press. The page illustrated above gives the learners background information about the French press before they start work on the French newspaper articles themselves. The

INFO TECH
Multimedia in language learning

newspaper articles in French are presented with help available to support the learners' reading.

Despite the simplicity of authoring packages, the time and organisational demands of multimedia production are challenging. Those teachers who develop materials enjoy the challenge and the reward of working in this area. The time they devote to making materials goes beyond what should be expected of the average teacher. Given the effort involved in producing work, it is sensible for teachers to collaborate on producing materials and to pool what is produced. A teacher who is too tired in a lesson to interact with a class because of time spent the night before on authoring might not be making the best use of his or her time.

LEARNER-PRODUCED MULTIMEDIA WORK

Learners need to use the target language if learning is to take place. This is achieved through speaking and writing activities which may already include more adventurous approaches such as project work and video production (see InfoTech 4, *Video in language learning* by Brian Hill). Multimedia simply takes these approaches a step further. Instead of learners working on projects on paper, they can create them with multimedia. This has some immediate gains. The first is the level of interest and motivation that learners get when they are able to create multimedia. Teachers are often surprised at the interest previously reluctant learners show in language learning when they are given the opportunity to produce multimedia work. Learners also benefit from producing work using a range of media. They can, for example, record themselves in the target language and add this to their work. Work done on producing multimedia can be linked very effectively to other uses of ICTs in the languages area. For example, learners can gather information for project work from the Web or from keypals using e-mail.

57

However, if you adopt this type of approach, it is important not to allow the ICT element of the work to overwhelm the linguistic study. If you do not carefully structure and manage the use of time, there is a danger that lesson time which should be spent on language learning ends up being used on ICT activities. The multimedia program must be seen as a tool to facilitate the production of work in the target language, and its use should not become an end in itself.

Work done in this area will help you to meet requirements placed on you to incorporate ICT work into your subject area to raise further levels of achievement and will bring important benefits to learners. The changes brought about by rapid developments in media technologies are transforming the way we communicate ideas and information. Given languages' central position in communication, we need to respond to those changes by acknowledging them in the type of learning experiences we give learners.

Finally, there is a pedagogical argument that learners benefit more from making multimedia than from using what others have created. The interactivity that designers build into educational multimedia may help learning, but not on the same scale as the interaction available to learners producing their own work. When making materials learners take information and create something with it. To do this effectively, they have to structure that information into something comprehensible and meaningful. In that process they turn information into personal understanding or knowledge, making learning more profound. However, for this to work you must be available to facilitate the process by supporting and guiding the learner.

58

Practicalities

How you set about getting learners to produce multimedia will depend on a number of factors which are discussed below.

Access to hardware and software

Despite major investment in computing in education, it is still difficult to get access to computers when you want to use them. In schools which have small clusters of computers in each classroom the carousel approach works well. Small groups of learners rotate between discussing and planning projects, gathering data and assembling work on the computer. This is effective because much of the real learning takes place away from the computer in the discussion, organisational and review stages. The computing stage is where all the preparation is consolidated.

Preparing your own multimedia is likely to benefit from access to a scanner for capturing images from paper and converting them into digital files. A digital camera is useful as digital photos can be taken and then transferred to the computer ready for use in multimedia work, although photo CDs can fulfil the

same purpose. In addition to having your photos on paper or as transparencies, you can have digital copies of the images put on a CD-ROM from which they can be readily accessed.

As far as software is concerned, a lot can be achieved with the standard applications most schools have available. These include: a word processor, presentation software, a drawing and photo-editing package. Multimedia authoring packages are more specialised, but even these are frequently part of a school's existing software.

ICT skills

Basic ICT skills are essential for work in this area. Initial teacher training programmes make ICT skills one of the core requirements for trainees. In-service teacher training schemes are also in place to help the rest of the profession reach similar standards. So whatever skill shortages there are currently in this area, these are improving. For learners, language classes are not the place for work on developing the basic ICT skills; these should be acquired in information technology classes.

59

Time

Although finding the time to complete any work done on computers will be challenging and will depend on the scale of the tasks you have set, there are ways to make this achievable. If learners have access to computers outside class time they can complete work during their free time or self-study periods. For some learners this will mean using the school computer room, self-access centre or library, the more fortunate learners can do this on a home computer. Another way of finding more time for this is to develop cross-curricular projects with teachers working in ICT, art and design, and perhaps geography and history. Time can then be found in these lessons for research or the creation of materials to go into a final project.

Planning

The central factor in completing any learner produced multimedia work successfully is good planning. The following questions will help you to control how the work progresses:

■   Why is the work being done in terms of the language learning outcomes?

- What aspect of the curriculum does it address?

- Who will be doing the work?

- Who will be available to support them?

- Where will the work be done?

- What stages are involved in getting the work finished?

- When will the work be done?

- When will it be finished?

- How will the work be assessed?

Put your answers to these down on paper and timetable everything.

Presentations

60

Presentation software is exciting for learners to use because it is simple to begin producing impressive work which is vivid in terms of colour, visuals and sound. Seeing work presented clearly and boldly motivates learners to get the language they use right. This type of software can be used to produce short presentations in the target language with accompanying visuals. Here are some ideas to experiment with:

- **This is me!**: a series of six slides in the target language in which the learners present themselves, their interests and their families with supporting illustrations.

- **Lexical sets**: you give a central theme, for example 'shops', pairs of learners then research lexical sets related to a subset of the theme, such as 'in the bakers'. Learners find or, if appropriate, create illustrations to support the vocabulary they are working on.

- **Dialogue builds**: pairs work together to write a dialogue. The theme and situation is determined by you. Having completed the preparation, the learners perform the dialogue using the presentation to check their performance or for prompting. This activity has great potential because the software allows the user to display a sentence at a time either automatically or by pressing the spacebar.

- **Story builds 1**: you give the learners a skeleton presentation. Each slide has an illustration. The learners have to create a story written directly onto the slides linking the pictures. Learners cross check each other's work for readability and accuracy.

- **Story builds 2**: a group of learners act out a series of tableaux for a story with one of them taking digital photos. The photos are transferred onto computer, incorporated into a presentation, and the story written up.

- **Famous people**: learners research a famous person from the target culture and create a short biography of the person using text and illustrations.

- **Comparison and contrast**: learners compare and contrast different aspects of their own and the target culture. The themes need not be complex, e.g. national sports, food, entertainment.

- **Preparation for a debate**: learners investigate one side of a debate and prepare a presentation to advocate the viewpoint they have researched. The presentations are used to initiate an in-class debate.

61

- **Product promotion**: learners are given a new product to sell in the target culture. They create a presentation promoting the product. This activity works well if an element of the ridiculous can be injected into it, e.g. promoting chip-butties as fast food in France.

- **Writing up a school trip**: learners write up a recent school trip.

These ideas are far from exhaustive and if you experiment with using presentation software, you are likely to come up with ideas which work more effectively with your learners and your style of teaching. Any completed presentations which follow a theme can be linked and then recycled with other groups. Given that presentation packages were developed to produce materials to accompany presentations, anything that learners create can be used by them to accompany an oral presentation. Whatever work is done with presentation packages, it is important that the learners' main focus is on effective and accurate use of the target language rather than mastery of the presentation package itself.

62

A screen from a learners' presentation on *Les grands milieux naturels du monde*

(© Derek Kelly, King Edward VI School, Southampton)

The illustration above is taken from a presentation produced by learners in a Year 9 French set. The teacher used work on the presentation to supplement a unit in the course book on *'l'environnement et ses problèmes'*. Pairs were asked to find a Website which dealt with one of the problems presented in class and then incorporated the information they found into a six-slide presentation. The exercise encouraged learners to focus on key language and vocabulary and integrated the language they acquired into a more comprehensive piece.

Multimedia authoring

The idea of learners producing multimedia work will seem unrealistic to teachers who have not yet tried it. For those who have, it becomes possible to foresee a time when it will become commonplace for learners to organise their ideas and notes, and to present their work in this format. This is particularly relevant to language learners because multimedia can record their written performance and their spoken ability too.

INFO TECH

Multimedia in language learning

The list of suggestions for work which can be done with presentation software applies equally to multimedia authoring packages. However, producing materials with authoring software means that the learners can be more inventive in how they present their work. By showing how the example activities presented above could be extended using multimedia authoring this should become clearer.

- **Lexical sets**: using presentation software, pairs of learners can work on vocabulary development by gathering and presenting the vocabulary associated with particular shops. With authoring software the learners can extend this by, for example, using a picture of a shop on screen and adding **hotspots** over significant vocabulary items. Clicking on these items will bring up the name of the object in a pop-up box. With another click a recording of the learner pronouncing the word could be played. If a number of groups in the class worked on different shops, the class would be able to produce several digital pages on one theme which could then be linked. The aim of this work is not the production of multimedia, but the embedding of vocabulary items in the learners' memories. This is built into this exercise through the creative effort the learners bring to the task.

63

- **Story builds**: with a multimedia authoring package a class can be given an initial scenario and opening to a story. Groups of learners then develop this by creating different possible outcomes. When these are linked to the opening, it makes a reading activity in the target language which can either be a 'reading maze' or a 'branching narrative'. As readers work through the final story, they can make choices at key points in the text, their choices leading to different conclusions. If the options available to the readers relate to choices of correct target language, then learners actually create meaningful learning tasks for their classmates.

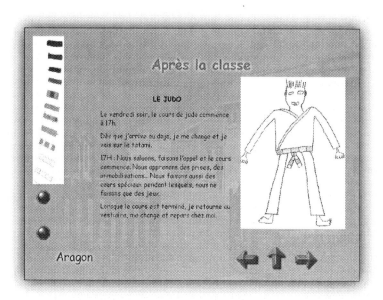

A screen from a multimedia project at l'École Aragon du Houlme, Normandie
Mon école en l'an 2000 (© Brighton & Hove LEA, Communauté de l'Agglomération Rouennaise)

The illustration above is taken from a multimedia project which linked three schools in Brighton and Hove, Sussex, and three in Rouen, Normandie. The aim of the project was to get the children to produce work which showed life in their schools and neighbourhoods. By putting all the projects together on a CD-ROM, the children in Sussex and Normandie are able to see the similarities and differences between children's lives in the two regions. The schools involved were all primary schools, but the children were, with teacher support, able to produce some effective multimedia.

Planning a project is demanding. At the Virtual Teacher Centre Website, in the section on ICT in the Curriculum and Modern Foreign Languages, there are a number of case studies which provide useful information on organising and running multimedia projects. (See Chapter 6 for the Website address.)

INFOTECH
Multimedia in language learning

The Web

Multimedia created by the teacher and learners for the Web is an important area. Working with the Web is now relatively easy because of the range of software available to help you produce work. The Web allows others to view your work and to collaborate with you in the production of work. Although the Web is a major multimedia area, it does not yet offer the same range of functionality or control that is available using the packages we have presented in this chapter. This area is covered in detail in InfoTech 3, *WWW The Internet* by Terry Atkinson.

65

6 Useful lists and information

ADDRESSES

Materials distributors

These distributors all supply language learning multimedia packages on CD-ROM and Computer-Assisted Language Learning software.

AVP
School Hill Centre,
Chepstow, Monmouthshire,
NP6 5PH.
Tel: 01291 625 439.
Fax: 01291 629 671.
E-mail: info@avp.co.uk.
Website: www.avp.co.uk

European Schoolbooks Ltd
Head Office and Warehouse:
The Runnings, Cheltenham,
Gloucestershire, GL51 9PQ.
Tel: 01242 245 252.
Fax: 01242 224 137.
E-mail: direct@esb.co.uk.
Website: www.eurobooks.co.uk/

Learning and Teaching Scotland
Glasgow Office:
74 Victoria Crescent Road,
Glasgow, G12 9JN.
Tel: 0141 337 5000.
Fax: 0141 337 5050.
E-mail: enquires@ltscotland.com.
Website: www.ltscotland.com/

Multimedia publishers
These companies both produce and distribute their materials.

Anglia Multimedia
PO Box 18,
Benfleet,
Essex, SS7 1AZ.
Tel: 01268 755 811.
Fax: 01268 755 811.
E-mail: scauk@aol.com.
Website: www.anglia.co.uk

Dorling Kindersley Ltd
The Penguin Group UK,
80 Strand,
London WC2R ORL.
Tel: 020 7010 3000.
Fax: 020 7010 6060.
E-mail: onlineDKcustomer.service@dk.com
Website: www.dk.com

EuroTalk Ltd
315–317 New Kings Road,
London, SW6 4RF.
Tel: 020 7371 7711.
Fax: 020 7371 7781.
E-mail: zannie@eurotalk.co.uk.
Website: www.eurotalk.co.uk

67

INFOTECH

Multimedia in language learning

Granada Learning Ltd
Granada Television, Quay Street,
Manchester, M60 9EA.
Tel: 0161 827 2927.
Fax: 0161 827 2966.
E-mail: info@granada-learning.co.uk.
Website: www.granada-learning.com

Language Intelligence
Pine View, Kingswood Road, Gunnislake,
Cornwall PL18 9DF.
Tel: 01822 832 975.
Fax: 01822 832 062.
E-mail: info@language-intelligence.co.uk.
Website: www.language-intelligence.co.uk

68

Vektor Ltd
The Oaks,
Preston Road,
Chorley,
Lancashire, PR7 1PL.
Tel: 01257 232 222.
Fax: 01257 234 039.
E-mail: info@vektor.com.
Website: www.vektor.com

Computer-assisted language learning software

Camsoft

10 Wheatfield Close,
Maidenhead,
Berks, SL6 3PS.
Tel/fax: 01628 825 206.
E-mail: info@camsoftpartners.co.uk.
Website: www.camsoftpartners.co.uk

INFOTECH

Multimedia in language learning

Half Baked Software
University of Victoria Language Centre.
Website: http://web.uvic.ca/hrd/halfbaked/index.htm
Publisher of *Hot Potatoes*

Wida Software Ltd
2 Nicholas Gardens,
London, W5 5HY.
Tel: 020 8567 6941.
Fax: 020 8840 6534.
E-mail: widasoft@lang.wida.co.uk.
Website: www.netkonect.co.uk/wida

Multimedia authoring packages

HyperStudio

69

TAG Learning Ltd,
25 Pelham Road,
Gravesend, Kent,
DA11 OHU.
Tel: 0800 591 262.
Fax: 01474 537 887.
Website: www.taglearning.co.uk

Junior MultiMedia Lab

Sherston Software Ltd,
Angel House, Sherston,
Malmesbury, Wiltshire,
SN16 OLH.
Tel: 01666 843 200.
Fax: 01666 843 216.
E-mail: sales@sherston.co.uk
Website: www.sherston.com

Illuminatus

INFOTECH
Multimedia in language learning

Digital Workshop,
43/44 North Bar Street,
Banbury, Oxon, OX16 OTH.
Tel: 01295 258 335.
Fax: 01295 254 590.
E-mail: sales@digitalworkshop.co.uk.
Website: www.digitalworkshop.co.uk/

Mediator

MatchWare Ltd,
Greyhound House, 23–24 George Street,
Richmond, Surrey, TW9 1HY.
Tel: 020 8940 9700.
Fax: 020 8332 2170.
E-mail: london@matchware.net.
Website: www.matchware.net/

70

INFOTECH

Multimedia in language learning

USEFUL WEBSITE ADDRESSES

BBC Learning Zone – Languages
www.bbc.co.uk/education/lzone/lang.shtml

BBC Bitesize – Education Revision
www.bbc.co.uk/education/schools/revision/

The British Educational Communications and Technology Agency (BECTA)
www.becta.org.uk/index.cfm

Becta reviews of CD-ROMs
www.becta.org.uk/information/cd-roms/

The Centre for Information on Language Teaching and Research (CILT)
www.cilt.org.uk

Eurotalk Interactive
www.eurotalk.co.uk/

Granada Learning
www.granada-learning.com/

Lingu@NET: Virtual Language Centre
www.linguanet.org.uk/material/material.htm

The National Grid for Learning
www.ngfl.gov.uk/index.html

The New Opportunities Fund – Education
www.nof.org.uk/edu/edu.htm

PEP International Directory of Educational Software Publishers
www.microweb.com/pepsite/Map/foreign.html

ReCall Software Reviews
www.hull.ac.uk/cti/resources/reviews/revlist.htm

The Virtual Teacher Centre
http://vtc.ngfl.gov.uk/

This has a useful section on Enhancing Modern Foreign Languages with ICT section including a multimedia authoring project at:
http://curriculum.becta.org.uk/docserver.php?temid=90

71

INFOTECH

Multimedia in language learning

GLOSSARY

Application
A computer program designed to be used for a particular purpose, e.g. a word processor for preparing documents.

CD-ROM
Compact Disk – Read Only Memory: A silver disk (12 cm) which holds a large amount of digital data (650 Mb). The disk is 'read only memory' which means that the data on the disk cannot be interfered with and no data can be added.

Concordancer
An application which searches a database of authentic text for occurrences of a word you have chosen and displays examples of the word in context.

Digital data
Data stored in digital rather than analogue format.

Digital files
Information whether text, image or sound stored on computer in digital format.

Digitising
Taking something in an analogue form and converting it into digital data. So, for example, taking a photo and converting it into a digital file using a scanner so it can be viewed on a computer, edited, printed out, saved and retrieved later.

DVD
Digital Versatile Disk: A storage medium with a huge capacity; ten times that of a CD-ROM.

Electronic networks
Telecommunications networks which allow digital data to be sent and accessed.

Floppy disks
(Or diskette) A small plastic disk which stores digital information (1.4 Mb)

Hardware
Hardware is all the electronic components of a computer system. It is generally used to talk about computers themselves and the pieces of equipment which are attached to them, including items like printers and scanners.

72

Hotspots	A word or graphic is 'hot' if by clicking on it additional information appears.
Hypertext	Similar to a hotspots. A system of inter-linking data so that by clicking on text, related or associated text or images can be viewed. This may be achieved by displaying a different section of the same page or by displaying a different page entirely. This process is commonly thought of as 'navigating'.
Installation	Before a software application can be used it must be installed on the computer. In this process files are transferred to the computer's memory.
Internet	A global system which allows computer users to exchange data and communicate with each other.
Package	See 'application'.
Scanner	A piece of equipment which digitises text, images or graphics so that they can be viewed, edited and stored on a computer.
Software	A computer program or application that allows the user to access and/or change data which is part of the program or which is supplied by the user.
Translation package	A software package which can produce a rough translation of a piece of text from one language to another.
Voice recognition	An application which enables a user to convert spoken language into text.
World Wide Web	Global system of electronic documents accessible via the Internet.

73

INFO TECH

Multimedia in language learning

REFERENCES

Atkinson T, *WWW The Internet* (CILT, 1998)

Buckland D, *Putting achievement first: Managing and leading ICT in the MFL department* (CILT, 2000)

Collin S, *Multimedia for Windows 95 Made Simple* (Made Simple, 1997)

Hewer S, *Text manipulation: Computer-based activities to improve knowledge and use of the target language* (CILT, 1997)

Hill B, *Video in language learning* (CILT, 1999)

Thompson J and Parsons J, *ReCALL Software Guide Number 4* (CTI Centre for Modern Languages, 1995)

Townsend K, *E-mail: Using electronic communications in foreign language teaching* (CILT, 1997)

74

Multimedia in language learning